Only So Far

Only So Far

R O B E R T   C O R D I N G

CavanKerry ◈ Press LTD.

CavanKerry Press Ltd.

Fort Lee, New Jersey

www.cavankerrypress.org

Publisher's Cataloging-in-Publication (Provided by Quality Books, Inc.)

Cording, Robert.
[Poems. Selections]
Only so far / Robert Cording. --
First edition.
pages cm
Poems.
ISBN 978-1-933880-49-5

I. Title.

PS3553.O6455A6 2015   811'.54
QBI15-600123

Cover painting © 2015 by Gray Jacobik
Cover and interior text design by Gregory Smith
First Edition 2015, Printed in the United States of America

NOTABLE VOICES
CavanKerry♦Press

CavanKerry Press is proud to publish the works
of established poets of merit and distinction.

CavanKerry Press is grateful for the support it receives from the
New Jersey State Council on the Arts.

Books by Robert Cording

For Muriel, Richard, and Ronald,

and in memory of Robert Koehne Cording

What is the meaning of life? That was all—a simple question; one that tended to close in on one with years. The great revelation had never come. The great revelation perhaps never did come. Instead there were little daily miracles, illuminations, matches struck unexpectedly in the dark.

—Virginia Woolf, *To the Lighthouse*

Ah, my deare angrie Lord,
Since thou does love, yet strike;
Cast down, yet help afford;
Sure I will do the like.

I will complain, yet praise;
I will bewail, approve:
And all my sowre-sweet dayes
I will lament, and love.

—George Herbert, "Bitter-sweet"

Contents

Kafka's Fence

I

II

III

Only So Far

Kafka's Fence

In a drawing by Kafka, a man stands behind a fence,
looking out. He could easily step over
the fence—it is that low—yet we imagine him
pacing back and forth like a prisoner.

The man could have just come to this boundary,
or been here his entire life. Call him Moses, and call
the land on the other side of the fence, Canaan,
and it doesn't matter how small the fence is, does it?

And you and I?—surely, we've spent a lifetime
arriving precisely at this fence. Haven't we
always known we'd reach an end we couldn't complete,
the promised land a step away, still unreachable?

I

Homeward

It's where I'm headed, that quaint word
in my head as my walk circles back
this late November day.
The sun's resigned to going down
earlier each afternoon. It sinks slowly
over the pond toward December's bottom.

When a truck passes, piled deep with cut wood,
it magnifies the longing in my body
for this cold, windy day to flame up.
Nostalgia: that cleaving to a childhood home;
or the way memory cleaves *return* and *home,*
so there's no getting home—only the remembering

of some happiness that went unrecognized
when, long ago, it was being had.
Fallen, and heaped up by the wind at the road's edge,
a windrow of pine needles seems pale as the clippings
of my childhood hair on the barber's floor.

Winter Evenings in Florida

Because Florida stretches the end
of our continent toward the equator,

the sun spends itself more lavishly
and, pilgrims, we follow that star

south, devoted to the light
of longer days and sunsets eager to please.

Each evening we arrive, right on time,
as if something momentous

were about to happen. And it does—
the day downshifts, the wind slackens,

the Gulf's green breathes and shines
with the sky's orange and pinkish-blues,

and the sun puts out a saucer of light
we lap like cats. It's a potion for forgetfulness

and, as day's end expands across the Gulf,
our bickering ideas of love and work,

our questions without answers, seem almost to lie
beyond recall. We feel instead

as if we're being given a vast truth,
the sight of something particular and complete,

which we'd like to put into words
but those, too, have been forgotten.

And now, what's left of the sun's gleaming
wake fast disappearing, we applaud

the loveliness of what's passing,
the ease of mind it brought so easily,

though already we wish our clapping
could summon an encore,

or help to conceal a sadness that puzzles us
as we disperse to the sound of car doors

shutting, and music turned up
too loud as we make our way home.

Still Listening

1. Hospice Jumble

The *Jumble* in the paper too hard for him to read,
my mother suggested we make up our own: Dear,

she said to her husband, your first word is *life*.
Reduced to words we jumbled, he joked *file*

it. My brother offered another, *mean*,
thinking perhaps of his diabetes, a *name*

like cancer to our family. Then, *lamp*,
lit at his bedside, and the one *palm*

visible outside his one windowed *room*.
My father got them quickly, the last, *moor*,

said with all the sadness of being far from *shore* . . .
A grandchild solved that one—*horse*,

she blurted, noticing that he had left
us for a while. By his bed, my mother felt

his hands and face and eyes. Bob, please,
she said, but he was already asleep,

snoring, not dead. My mother sighed, O God.
My brother, in the spirit still, said dog.

2. Near the End

"sometimes old people snap back into life"

—*A. R. Ammons*

My father gave up dreams early on:
too much damage in them.
He never thought much of choices either,
deferring until something chose him—
the army, a wife, a job. He was
always withdrawing from the world
even as he went about his life in it.

From his hospital room we watched
the clouds sag, the sun go down;
at night, cars crawled by outside
with their headlights on. Before
became After. Each day it took him
longer and longer to become a man
again. So it was with surprise,

when, near the end, death already
in the room, my father snapped back
into life for a few weeks, making plans
to attend a grandson's wedding,
having my mother rearrange his dialysis
around the celebration. Then, After
became Before again: he remembered
how he couldn't walk, how he couldn't
see or hear, and waited painfully

and without volition for the cup
of nothing-left-to-enjoy to come
his way. And when it did,
what else could he do but drink.

3. My Father's Coma

Like a cave-in deep in a mine,
my father's stroke,
his mouth hanging open an entry
to a bewildering underworld
where there was no chance
of enlightenment or journey.

Listening to the sounds
he produced was like listening
to the last muffled tapping
of a trapped miner to cease.
And then the man we called
father and *husband* was dead,
his mouth still gaping
as if his corpse was letting out
a last scream that none of us
could hear—a silence
for which we are still grateful.

4. What My Father Said

God is still speaking, but we're not listening,
the sign in front of the church proclaims,

one of those little witticisms to jar us
out of the habitual trance of commuting
along the same daily route, driving to work,
or bringing the kids to school, and it gets me
thinking of my recently dead father

who, when my mother nagged him
from another room, *are you sleeping again,*
you better wake up if you're sleeping,
do you hear me? answer me, would respond,
now that he'd been roused from another
head-pitched-forward, mouth-open,
elbow-slipping-from-the-bar-of-his-walker-
snooze, *I hear you, but I'm not listening.*

5. My Father's Hearing Aids

Too costly to throw out,
my mother says; my father's hearing aids,
some whole, some in various stages
of disassembly, lie in his top drawer
like a museum exhibit of a lost past—
when he was still living,
hand constantly raised to his ears,
trying to take hold of the sounds
that fell out of the air or floated
around him like apparitions.

I fit one into my ear
as if, my own hearing amplified,
I might pick up something he is

still saying, but all I get is that loud hum
and screech, which, like a rip
in the scrim of memory,
bring him back—he's at it again,
working to tune in the scramble
of insect chirr, rain chattering
on the trailer's metal roof,
wind in the pines, a grandchild's
high-pitched play, the buzz
of his wife's voice. He wants to hear

again without thinking
of what he's hearing, wants the Sinatra
song on the radio to sound exactly
the way he remembers it,
and not as if some damaged stylus
were sliding across the black ice
of an old LP. In the end,
nothing ever came to him clearly enough.

I see him spinning those little dials
on his hearing aids back and forth,
nearly frantic, nearly in tears,
the world he's hearing
like the static of space, those gurgling,
stuttering, anomalous noises
we have our radar pointed at
as if we cannot imagine, being human,
the deep, enclosing silence
without another voice.

Amnesty

You're huddled in your coat, waiting
at the corner for the sign—
a little walking man—
to give the go-ahead, the numbers,
already descending, counting down
the time left for a safe crossing.

And even if you look both ways,
and still wish to see beyond your seeing,
you have only these twenty seconds,
as you walk from one side to the other
late in the day, to catch the ideal
angle of the sun entering the notch

between buildings, and enamelling just now
the high windows and soffits
in cloisonné glimmerings; to enjoy
this little amnesty of not thinking
if you've been given enough or too little.

Belated Elegy, January 1, 2011

for Peace Pilgrim, 1908–1981

On this day in 1953 you began to walk.
It's a new year once again, and I need
to hope that your story says more
about the mystery of love than my fear
of self-sacrifice, and the indifference
of history. You died about the time
I was ready to believe in something other
than the fruited plains of shopping malls
and the rhetoric of desire papered
on billboards. You saw a country hurtling
forward on retail dreams, and lies
about the necessity of war, and decided
to live your life as a declarative sentence:

I'll walk for peace. For 28 years, you did,
one little person, giving all her time for peace.
You believed others would give some
of their time, and history would be made—
History, who never finishes a sentence,
and speaks in dependent clauses,
always arriving at new wars. You crossed
our country eight times, logged over
70,000 miles to *overcome evil with good,*
falsehood with truth, hatred with love.
You simply lived into the future you wanted.
It's that simplicity that terrifies me.

You never spoke against the machine
of money I hate, how it keeps fingering
every untouched next new market. Or how
we separate our words from deeds
to push our plans of self-aggrandizement.
The way of peace is the way of love
is all you'd say. Walking into town
in your blue pants, your sweatshirt
declaring you PEACE PILGRIM, you could
have been anyone's grandmother
moving among us. We thought
giving you a meal or a place to sleep
was all that was required.

History appears to have had the last word:
you, killed in a car crash after accepting
a ride. You'd wanted to be on time
for a talk you were to deliver—"Attaining
Inner Peace by Giving Up Your Life"—
the irony almost impossible to believe.
I'd like to dismiss your simple-minded act
and thereby excuse myself in a poem
for my lack of action, but I cannot
stop thinking about how the wars keep
adding up, and how what should be
intolerable keeps becoming what is usual
and expected and so much easier
to live with than the love you walked for.

Like a Dream

In patches of sunlight, they rise
through the green water like small clouds
or hang suspended a few feet below
the surface like a dream being remembered—

manatees, so calmly slow and bovine,
they seem lobotomized by the engines
of our hurry as we race over them, their bodies
bearing the marks of our impatience.

Have they made some placid truce
with our noisy world above them,
unable to do more than what they do?—rise
to the surface, their buoyant peace

a kind of offering and sacrifice,
a story to be told thousands of years from now
on some cathedral wall—of creatures that passed
beneath us, at rest in their movement,

then disappeared from our world,
never needing anything from us,
their peace only able to bear us so far,
even if we always wanted to believe in it.

Outside my window, four palm trees
shake their mop-tops in the windy cold
like they're the Beatles, and it's 1964 . . .
and I'm fifteen, stretched out before the altar
of a console TV, the wooden doors opened
because it's Sunday, and television is allowed,
recompense for early morning attendance
at church. My father reads the paper,
something, no doubt, about JFK's assassination,
and perhaps the rumors of the war to come
in southeast Asia. My mother sews.
And just when I think Sullivan cannot speak
any more slowly, he lets out the magic words
"youngsters from Liverpool," and the audience explodes
and the night accelerates and the Beatles'
"All My Loving" fills our living room,
and I'm looking at Paul looking at John,
and even they can't believe what is happening.

What is happening?—I've forgotten tomorrow
is Monday, forgotten the north Jersey sky
outside our door, and how, starless
and alien, it's always tinged with green
from a neighbouring electric plant;
I've forgotten the tedious blocks
of 50 x 100 lots, and the ranch houses
with four basic floor plans we all live in.
The Beatles are in our living room,
and whatever is happening includes me

when Paul smiles his isn't-this-cool,
isn't-this-nuts smile. I'm shaking
my head, trying to make my too-short hair
spill around my face, and I'm beginning
to think the world I know isn't the only one.

And when the Beatles go right into
"She Loves You," I'm all *Yeah, Yeah, Yeah,*
so far outside my usual self
I let my father's complaints about the lyrics
slip by uncommented on. And even now,
forty years later, I can see their smiling faces.
We're all there in the living room,
my mother humming along, my father
lost behind the Sunday papers, and me,
unimaginably free, shaking myself alive,
summoned into a future knowing so little
and wanting so much, armed with
nothing more than joy and wonder.

December 17, 1831

I know what he wrote about it,
but this cold morning I'm thinking about
how long it must have taken
de Tocqueville to sort out what he came upon
that morning, the sky a washed-out cloth,
the sun flat-lined along the black and white horizon . . .

I suppose the Frenchman was looking for words
even then, trying to describe the sound of drums
that had come toward him,
the whinnying of unseen horses, and then
a whole tribe of Choctaw Indians bursting
from the woods, led by Federal agents.

When he swallowed, the freezing December air
must have been a lump in his throat.
I see blocks of ice swirling in the Mississippi,
following the current's one-way directive,
and an old woman—over a hundred,
de Tocqueville thought—who wanted to stay
right there and die on the only land she'd ever known.
But the Indians, all of them, were politely herded
onto a steamboat, the signal given to push off.

Writing about that day years later,
he remembers its quiet orderliness,
the New World he liked to praise
shipping off an older world already here,
but doing so with the reasonableness of law.

Then his sentences, considered,
full of modifications, turn to the way
the Indians' dogs, left behind, barked, then howled
and kept on howling long after the boat
had departed, and in his head long after that.

Buying a TV

I'm carting a 55-inch flat-screen
to the car when I'm surprised
by sounds I haven't heard
for some time and can't believe
I'm hearing here—the nasally *peent, peent*
of a woodcock broadcasting its call
from the fields beside this new Wal-Mart.
And then I see the male's sloping
upward spiral, its wings chittering
as it rises, no more than a speck now,
and the chirping circle it makes
at its apex, before it tumbles down,
zigzagging like a blown leaf.
I want to exclaim "Hark" out loud
in the middle of the parking lot,
and stop the guy loading his car
with bags of mulch, but the bird,
rising up again, is barely visible
against the horizon of clouds
that could be, just now, English hills
where some Romantic reconnects
to what's been missing from his life.
I tell myself this display's
not for the guy driving off, or for me,
or anyone for that matter,
but just a bird doing what a bird does
with spring inside him. Besides,
what I'm seeing—and I can barely admit this—
would be a lot more spectacular

on one of those Planet Earth shows
in 1080 HD. Yet here I am,
unable to turn away. It's late
in the day, the sun's lowered
its hold, and the parking lot's rinsed
in twilight colors. I'm trying to explain
to myself why a bird I can hardly see
has cracked me open ever so slightly,
as if, standing here, stopped
on the way to the car like one
of Wordsworth's 19th-century travelers,
I've been re-living the memory
of another place, long lost.

Tonight, our spoonful of uplift
is red-crowned cranes, wings up,
legs down, floating into the DMZ
on the feel-good spot of the news.

It's almost a sanctuary, the reporter says,
this open, empty land that runs along
the 38th parallel between North
and South Korea for 160 miles. It's true,

the cranes have found refuge here,
the land, people-less, littered with mines
and surrounded by troops, left behind
to the birds for the time being.

It's almost comical how the report
shuffles between an opportunistic nature
rushing in to fill an emptiness,
and the vague sense of some power

larger than us fixing once again
what we've broken. I'm no better.
I'm dragging up Camus, yes, Camus,
who wondered how we could ever be

miserable, so much beauty in the world,
but, also, how we could ever be happy,
so much shit in the world. I'd have him
do the voiceover for this final montage—

a new day, the morning sun oranging
the snow-dusted marsh, the camera closing in
on a pair of cranes, their necks dipping,
rising, one head bowing to the other until

the pair lift into air as if they are levitating,
then fall, their wings opened like parachutes
as they touch down ever so lightly on the earth
where all that poised firepower waits.

The Restorer

After hours, maybe you knock down
three or four too many scotches
and go pagan at some distant neighborhood's
karaoke bar, holding your crotch like Morrison
as you give it up for *Light My Fire*.
But right now, in this basement room
of the museum, you seem content
with the freedom of confinement, happy
to give up notions of how things might have been
if only you'd had more ambition or talent.

It's hard to believe the extravagance
of your restraint, the way you've escaped
the hellish flames of possibility, the twists and turns
of having to choose one thing over another.
You must have spent years undergoing
some ancient discipline of breathing and posture
to gain the unhurried calm it takes
to match someone else's colors. I'm startled
by your lack of need, the way you follow another's
lead into the painting, another Dutch landscape

of margins—land and sea, sea and sky,
a single walker and a distant windmill that enlarges
the vast stretch of a fogged in morning.
After hours of considering, you dab grays in
here and there, restoring some nearly lost balance,
glad you could tie up a few loose ends.

You could be part of the landscape you are restoring,
these undulating wetlands at the edge of the sea,
the lone walker disappearing in gray mist,
a man like you without a name.

Mid-Winter, Florida

In cold and snow, forced to huddle inside
like a small animal in a hole
among the roots of trees—so the mind,
with nothing to look at, and retelling
old stories to itself, planted a suggestion:
this trip, mid-winter, to Florida . . .

where the horizon of morning lifts
inch by inch at the window,
and a mockingbird unlatches the day.
Last night's rain hangs in the leaves
of a live oak, but the sun lifts each drop
into crystalline light, the air gravity-free.

And now my mind, looking to speak
this new language of *now, now, now,*
floats out the window, free again,
and focuses on one thing after another—
this turtle lost in the clouds drifting
on the flat surface of the pond,
and then the communal will of sandpipers
rising and turning all at once above the water.

And now, on a stucco wall, the gaiety
of shadows thrown by a hibiscus, its extravagant
silk-skirt blooms blowing in a breeze
off the Gulf, my skin shivering with pleasure.

II

"Essence"

I'm listening to Lucinda Williams long
for her lover's essence,
her half sob, half sigh a reminder
of how I, too, am always longing
for something that is somewhere else,
something that is part of me
and yet something else entirely . . .

And now I'm remembering my college crush
on Teilhard de Chardin, who could not believe
all our longings went to waste,
and so collected them in a noosphere
of consciousness that wrapped the earth,
and was part of a universe
always evolving toward higher levels
of consciousness, aimed
at an Omega Point that drew us
not just onwards, but upwards
toward itself, like Christ who drew
all things into himself—a completeness
Lucinda and I have always wanted,
but can never enter completely.

It's what Lucinda wants *now*,
her lover's essence a drug,
a gift shot directly into her, a breath
she can feel on her face,
but when she takes up her song's refrain
one last time, I hear again

longing's hard counterpoint—
Baby, sweet baby, I'm waiting here for more,
waiting by your door, waiting on your back steps . . .
waiting for your essence.
And then, hunger unabated,
she lets even the words go,
her song becoming the lonely wail
of the guitars and the essential one-two,
one-two of the drums that give
a heartbeat to our never-satisfied needs.

Bede's Sparrow

In the middle of the day, I was lost
in thought, staring at my newly dead father,
or the portion of him the funeral home
gave me back in a cheap little plastic urn
I'd placed on my study's mantle.
I'd been reading about Bede's sparrow,
which, it turned out, was not Bede's at all,
but a story he wrote down, told by
some anonymous advisor to a king
in Northumbria who wondered if Christianity
offered something more specific
than the blank he'd drawn regarding the life
before and after the one he was living.

When I lapsed into the half-sleep
of daydream, I saw, behind my shut eyes,
my father and me in a mead hall, watching
a sparrow's darts and swoops. My father,
who had nothing to say now that he'd died—
no philosophy or theology, no joke even
about a man who walked into a mead hall—
kept his one good eye on the sparrow that flew
in one door and all too quickly out the other.

I wanted more, a replay in slow motion
at least, the sparrow's acrobatics up close,
the swooping loop-de-loops and slaloming,
the certainty of its last choice tinged with
the silvery-blue winter twilight,

but my father, who always said to my woes,
want less, turned his attention
to the emptiness of the door, the sparrow
now here, now gone, what you see,
what you can't, all the same to him.

He warmed himself by the fire,
and motioned to me. I half-expected
our old heated talk to resume,
my father tossing his beliefs my way,
beliefs I too often rejected as slogans
when he was alive—"things come at will
and not when you will them"—
but we are silent, my father wanting no more
than for me to sit with him and watch
the arabesque of flames,
as if that alone could take care of everything
I still so desperately needed.

Angel

Yesterday's tragedy is today's entertainment
on YouTube. Less than a day old,
this two-minute clip from last night's news
has over a million hits. Everyone's watching
Angel, a seventy-eight-year-old man hit by
a car that sped away, lying in the street
in downtown Hartford, blocks from
the Capitol dome, the half-gallon of milk
he was carrying broken on the pavement.
It's lunch-time, a cloudless summer day,
pigeons moping on the sidewalks, passersby
carrying off Styrofoam cartons of take-out.

What's got everyone watching is the number
of pedestrians who come to the curbside, look,
and rush away, hands in their pockets,
heads down, now and again looking back.
Two send a text to a friend, another
takes a picture on her cell. Six continue to wait
for their bus, watching as cars carefully
half-circle the elderly man, then zip away.

And there is someone whom we cannot see,
who filmed this street full of people and sold it
to the local station. And here I am,
replaying this scene, counting the people
on the street as if each one of them bears
some failure of my own. And there's that
ghostly bruise of milk leaking out like some kind
of divine substance, a would-be revelation.

Childhood Room

Always the same, even when it changed—
alive with rain and snow, with sunlight
and the moon. On a pair of shelves:
my books, my soldiers. Arranged
on the topmost limbs of a tree with leaves
shaped like hearts, small birds that flitted
in and out of sight. My parents' voices
talking in an adjacent room late at night.

Then dreams of my mother or father dead—
and awakened, my room not my own, I'm crying.
Then nights when I would not close my eyes,
when fear had me sitting upright in bed,
when my parents' assurances felt like lies.
Then words—*tulip, warblers, love, missing.*

Words

for Anne Ferry, 1930–2006

Sometimes, in the quiet before language comes,
I think of you, and of our class
clumped around the table,
December's early dark at the windows
as we waited for you to finish reading
Herbert's poem about his words
running amok, feverish in their straining ardor.

I take some comfort thinking of your voice
and the way you found the right words
to make the poem emerge,
slowly at first, and then all at once,
until we found ourselves able to speak
about the connections words awaken,
or feel the largeness of something not yet

given a name. Your voice had a body,
small and fierce and gentle,
and I can almost hear it, how your words
rowed me across the river of dark
each poem is. I am still listening. Listening
for what?—for the way a poem waits
in silence to be heard?

It pains me to think of how your gift
was so suddenly lost, words *unfindable*
(your husband's word) ever again.

There are no words for the unsuspected place
at which you arrived. So much that is
impossible to name, that remains a mystery
on the tip of the tongue, a blank stare.

Sometimes the poems you taught me
help me to know what it means to be here,
or who it is I am—not entirely, of course,
but helpful nevertheless—as if your voice
were again speaking to me, bringing into focus
what I didn't know I knew, wordlessly
giving me the words I need to speak.

Last Day

Two floors below, the oil burner rumbled on
inside the muffled sounds of the winter dream
I was waking from, our room unusually cold,
the windows iced. It was the last day of March.

A single mourning dove insisted, it seemed,
on being heard—its call, in my half-sleep,
and dampered by the window and its storm,
sounded like *where are you, you? where are you, you?*

You were in Chicago with your mother, and I knew,
or seemed to know right then, at the beginning
of the day, and long before you called at its end,
that the death you had gone home to wait for

would happen that day. And I thought of you
sitting with your mother, smoothing her hair,
giving her a sip of water, she nearly beyond being
a mother when you now felt most her daughter;

I thought of how your mother had carried you
inside her as she prepared your older brothers
and sisters for their day, drove to the store,
made dinner, talked with your father before sleep.

And then of how someone must have said
at the moment of your birth, *it's a girl,*
and your mother must have held you and kissed you
and called you for the first time by your name.

Annunciation

Just as you always have,
twice this week you called your mother,
the familiar numbers pushed
before you remembered
she was dead, a month already.
Yesterday, after you'd listened
to the telephone's unanswered ringing,
you told me how you saw
your mother's still unsold house,
the kitchen where the phone is,
all six chairs tucked in
around the table, and circled by
the ivy-trellised garden
the wallpaper makes.
I found you in tears,
in our kitchen, as if you were lost
or injured, the phone held to the side
of your head like a bandage,
and I thought of Mary
the moment after the angel leaves,
fully recognizing the future
that being loved will bring.

Realometer

In one of the longest sentences in *Walden,*
Thoreau puts one foot down, then the other,
in the slippery mud of inherited opinions;

and if the mud in his metaphor stands for
the muddle, say, of the theology of business

that keeps inventing the means to account
for its unjustifiable loose ends,

or for the hierarchy of religions that too often fight
for the singular rightness of their one
sum-of-it-all Idea,

it also suggests the fenny quagmire
of clichéd ideas on which one takes a pratfall,

unsettling what was thought to be settled
and landing the upstanding *I* on his ass—

who, once leveled, may have a good laugh
over the folly of never having recognized the Half-of-It
that dons the mask of All

before getting back up on his own
two feet, realizing that the time has finally come

to give up all his ploys, to reject the too-ready
language he wields in reality's name;

and now, if his Realometer can find the *This*
of solid rock, he might just be thankfully surprised
by how comfortably he can stand there.

I've been given a cabin on the Gulf and six weeks
to make sense of what's eluded me
for sixty-one years. Each day: a worrying
into words. Last night I stood on the beach
and looked out at the Gulf, then up
at the Milky Way and the two Bears
and then at my little cabin, with its two
dusty windows, and its light on the table
where I left my books and my notes
for poems—it was enough to clarify
what I would and would not accomplish.

★

"I really don't know any other way
of trying to make sense of my life,"
Penn Warren wrote to his old friend Allen Tate
in his seventies, enclosing a draft of a poem,
some new words to catch what was lost
the moment it occurred. The morning here is
one thing, then another—rain, sun, fog,
the light on the water grey, green, silver-blue.
Clouds settle in, then lift. The air's granular,
then clear. There's a pattern
in these scatterings, and there isn't.

★

I've been watching a fisherman casting out
and reeling in for hours, nothing to show
for his time. When someone asks
if he's caught anything, he replies—
"I'm hopeful"—and I think of the psychologist
on the radio the other night, explaining
our incessant need to check our inbox.
Intermittent Reinforcement, he called it,
adapting language for the behavior
of lab rats. Once food is placed in
their maze on random days, they can't
stop looking for more; like us, he said,
once an email has brought good news.

*

The tide's going out, and the sand,
washed clean, could be a Zen garden plot
ready to quiet all thought in silence.
The fisherman has broken down his rods
and carries them off now in an empty bucket,
happy enough, it seems, with his few hours
of meditative practice. I used to worry
about running out of words for things.
Now I worry I won't use up all the words
I've been given. Here, in my ill-lit cabin,
shadows moving across the walls,
I live for that poem or two that seem
to gather from the world, or my mind,
or both, what they have to give.

A Beginning

When an older friend slipped me in the side door
of a once grand pre–World War theater,
the first thing I saw were breasts, roundly dangling,
held out for me to admire by a blonde
on the screen who knew how to juggle her assets:
coming attractions. A voiceover narrator cooed,
what a sumptuous mass of pulchritude,
and my eyes worked to memorize what I was sure
would be taken away all too soon. And was,
as if by the impatient shouts of some older guys
who'd seen enough and urged on the main feature.

Nothing was ever enough for them.
If there was kissing and touching, they shouted,
we didn't pay for this; if a woman took off her bra,
they yelled, *show us your pussy.* Then, *give it to her
harder, take her from the rear*—as if they needed
the people on the screen to obey their orders.
Slowly, I began to see the women's faces—
how, bent over, tongues licking lips, their eyes
held no emotion, their cries of *oh, God!*
oh, God! Sweet Jesus, Yes! as rote as the sermons
I was forced to listen to each Sunday.

And those bodies going through the motions
were positioned, even to a virgin like me,
all wrong, too high or low. None of it was real.
Only those men, who hooted and whistled,
whom I imagined at their day jobs, cursed out

for not working fast enough or being smart enough.
I knew how they brought their smallness home.
Once, our backdoor neighbor screamed at his wife,
you'll fuck me when I tell you to, as he hurled
every one of her new dishes into the driveway.

And then I was back on the streets that were home
to loan sharks and a small-time mafia,
where my family shopped for canned goods
in someone's stocked garage, so much back then
falling off of trucks for us. In my head,
amid the babble of mixed messages, I was finding
words for the thrill of those breasts, each word
a match among cans of gasoline, my conflagration
burning down the going-out-of-business stores,
then the high school where I was always afraid,
where one-eyed Joey Zagaro stood up in class
and cursed out our teacher for calling on him;

but when my firestorm blazed down Main Street,
rushing toward the theater with its galaxy
of mythic gods circling the tattered ceiling,
I remembered the mortals below—men
whom I'd sat among and who knew too well
who they were and were not, motes of dust
shaking in the light of the screen, each of us
summed up in an equation for need and control,
nothing more commanding than those breasts,
super-sized, out of reach, *sumptuous.*

Evolution

We didn't have names.
Or, to be more exact, each of us
was called by the same name
in that nightly world
of conveyor belts that rolled
from basement to main floor
with boxes of soap powder, juice,
paper towels, and toilet paper.

It was *pay attention, you fucking whore,*
or *faster, you fucking whore,*
the damp stub of an unlit cigar
moving more than the lips
of our boss, Tony,
so short and squat, it seemed
as if something must have been
pressing down on his head for years.

I was seventeen, shouldering
the bafflement of what it meant
when relatives said,
I was becoming a man; I read poetry
in my spare time, and believed
Blake and Whitman were telling me,
and only me, I had to create myself.
Even in the gray fluorescent light
of the basement, I was always
heading for a better future. I could be

watching a mouse nose the crumbs
of a spilt bag of chips and still imagine
myself driving out of town, past the used
car lots, and all-night titty bars.

And so the time came—after I'd won
over my suffering night-shift brothers
by referring to Tony as one
of those lost *Time-Life* apes
that never quite evolved to become
part of the human family;
and after I'd joked that his only
survival tool, not quite language,
was his cursing and the ability to outlast
all of us by going nowhere;
and after he goaded me, my arms
trembling from fatigue
at the top of the conveyor belt, saying
I was *a fucking woman,*

I did what I thought any man would,
or any man who thought
tougher was safer,
or hadn't yet thought through
how he was part of a problem
he didn't yet know the extent of,
and pushed a box of six thirty-two-ounce
bottles of apple juice off the belt
and watched as they exploded
on the floor near where Tony stood,

all of him covered in little shards
of glass and juice, his little cigar falling
to the floor. And then I was out
the door, desperately trying to believe
I was in charge of my life,
just as I know now Tony must have
tried to believe all those nights.
The pale, drivelling, pre-dawn sky
was already streaked with the dirty smoke
of the coffee factories on Grand Avenue.

Indian Pipe

Paramour of shadows, of the dark under
beech and oaks, it appears out of nowhere
on some gray nothing afternoon you fill in
with a walk: *Ghost-Flower, Fairy Smoke.*

As if fashioned out of snow or rime
in these rain-soaked first weeks of summer,
it raises itself all at once, suddenly here—
Ice-Plant—like some lost fact that passes
from memory back into life.

Indivisible from the ring of roots
it grows above, it reigns over the rich harvest
of understory rot, living by what lies buried.
Broker of the in-between, of what is and is not,
its affront to color, its scaly, waxen white,
tilts the equilibrium of your summer self.

Picked, it blackens like a corpse.
And so it is forgotten until, here again,
its cool phallus reminds you of all
you do not wish to think about.

Sunset Time in Florida

It's winter at home, but here the magical sun
toppling into the Gulf abracadabras Happy Hour
at a local bar with a view of the water
where pocket-size waves ripple
with the tropical fish colors of a sun
waving goodbye to a round of applause.

Escapees from a literature convention, we watch
florid men go by in shirts with little palm trees
and women with matching pastel tops
and bottoms. We're still on our first drink
when we discover what we have in common
is our singular complaint: we're sixtyish

and invisible, though once we were
at least assured a gaze. We're both married,
she less happily so, or so I take her story
about an affair to mean, though it could be
a general unhappiness, the gap never closed
between the world she planned to live in

and the one she's living in. It's clear
that neither of us wants sex, just the titillation
of being desired. For anything to happen
we'd each have to be someone else.
Who she is becomes clearer when she moans
how her unhappiness is a failure to be happy.

She's feeling bad about feeling bad,
when I order us a second round, and say,
professorially, something stupid about
how no one makes the most of their chances,
and quote *Lear,* my go-to line when Gloucester
says mistakenly, "no worse, there is none,"

not yet realizing the worse to come.
She looks at me as if I'm rapidly becoming
part of her problem, so I toast the after-bloom
of light, a sunny tomorrow, and the enterprise
of a good night's sleep, sidestepping Hamlet's
thoughts of the indignities the flesh is heir to.

Fall Cleaning, Windows Mostly

I'm taking a break, slumped over,
a comic Rodin, my head resting in my hand,

when, looking down, I find it, fear-frozen
to an inch of warm floor by the radiator.

Does it see me? The mouse never budges.
A baby, I let it be, forget all about it,

but, hours later, notice it has not moved.
It's just thumb-sized, a dusky grey-brown.

I kneel down to eye it, examining the whiskers
that help it nose its way in the dark.

I cannot keep from touching
the soft malleable flesh I've seen shrink

under a baseboard or through a hole
I never even noticed.

And then I realize the mouse is dying,
and, minutes later, has died,

when I nudge it with my finger
and the mouse simply falls on its side,

no wound or sign to give its death
a reason. I don't know why,

as tenderly as a father, I hold it
in the palm of my hand—wouldn't I,

before the winter was up, have baited a trap for it?
Nor why, suddenly a pallbearer

for a mouse I would have killed,
I carry it outside and scoop a grave

with my hand in the hardening dirt
of the garden. I even feel the need to testify

(is it the shock of how briefly it was,
then was not?) to the unlucky hand

it was dealt. And now, hours after
I've tamped dirt over its body,

and gone back to washing windows,
I find myself mindlessly wiping

and re-wiping the glass,
as if I could turn each twelve-paned sash

into a portal of sheer transparency.

Elegy for an Idea

homage to Philippe Petit

September again, and again
I think of you,
and of what losses and disasters

the future holds. You believed
for us, and made us believe,
at least for a moment, that life

in the clouds can indeed be
grander, fuller, than the lives
we organize on earth.

You were our necessary fool,
and we delighted in your wit—
how calmly you walked

toward the waiting police
and then turned, just out of reach,
toward the opposite tower.

Eight times you crossed the wire
you'd strung between those
gleaming buildings, until even

the ones supposedly in charge
smiled and watched the sway
and counter-sway of your dance,

handcuffed by joy, pure and impartial.
Even now the images are dizzying—
you, with no defense but your gaiety,

in the void between the towers,
dwarfed by a plane overhead,
the tiny Statue of Liberty a souvenir

off in the background, all of it
the vast stage of your street magic
in the sky. There you are,

conjuring a theater out of the air,
a congregation of onlookers—
turned from their coffee and papers,

from the goods of store windows
and the absent reflections of themselves—
newly sighted by your procession

of concentration and delight,
by the sight of you kneeling
to the gods of the wind and the wire

you made into a hammock
when you chose to lie down
and talk with a circling gull

as if the world's secret wholeness
lay in just these rare interludes
of nonsensical communion.

III

The Field

I have often been afraid to think
of Augustine thinking, his mind a field,
he confesses, that must be worked with much cost
and sweat, and he the farmer laboring.

Just knowing how little one can know
is enough for most, but not Augustine—
whatever crept around in his mind had no right
to privacy. He kept on harrowing

himself, turning the dark soil to the sun.
He was often overcome by the strangeness
of his memory, which could remember
what he had lost, or at least forgotten—

a happiness he knew was surely real,
even if he had no way of knowing it
until it took root in the soil he was preparing.
I have often counted the efforts I've taken—

meditation, daily prayer, self-examination—
thinking I was preparing my own field.
And yet when I think of Augustine, I know
just how self-satisfied I have been,

that field so much vaster than my little self,
so much richer if only I could truly begin
the harrowing work, if only I could remember
the harvest Augustine knew was always waiting.

Pelicans

Last evening, another sunset party:
drinks, laughs, ironies, hidden desires.
All of us tanned and glowing, we exchanged
jokes and gossip, fresh and stale, self-conscious
that something larger was missing
when we turned to best watches, shoes, cigars.

So much time is lost trying to agitate
the envies of others and monitor one's own—
the thought that crossed my mind as I watched
six pelicans rise and fall with the water's flux.
The winds had quieted, and just before the sun plunged
below the sea, the pelicans rose in a wind-hung line

and flew off, silent as a council of gods
in the pinkish sky. Palm trees scratched
their cuneiform shadows on the sand.
I wanted to say something about the pelicans,
which I knew, for no known reason, choose to live
their lives as near total mutes, as if they've decided

simply to be done with the fecklessness of speaking,
but I kept quiet, the light draining from the sky,
the others going inside. I felt like a child in hiding,
alone on the deck, made fearful and alive
by the darkened Gulf, the stretch of beach
now entirely empty, the palm trees,

the sliver of moon rising directly opposite
of where the sun had set. If I had been called
to come in, I would have kept silent.

Arrival of the Gods

The gods are all around us, even now,
our imperious, bell-bottomed professor said,
half-heard, half-seen.

We half expected them. It was 1969.

Our class had studied the old myths,
and we were carrying out some ritual
of our teacher's invention

to dilate our narrow modern lives
so we might see the gods again
in rocks and trees and birds.

We needed drugs,

or at least a joint to pass around
as we sat cross-legged in a circle
under the quadrangle's oak tree.

We listened carefully, breathed, heard
the sound of oak leaves filling
the silence. The day

went down like a flaming plane.

I tried to smell burnt offerings
in smoke that wafted from a charcoal grill
somewhere down the street.

Now, now, our teacher chanted
to bring Orpheus singing.
Some found him

in a long-haired guitar player
scolding anyone who would listen
with Dylan's "Masters of War."

The war went on beyond our seeing.

We watched the wind blow
dust gods across the trampled,
nearly grassless quadrangle.

Class was dismissed. Our professor
strode away, an Olympian
indifferent to what had taken place

down below. I never looked back,
believing I'd find my Eurydice,
full-fleshed, in front of me

in the cafeteria line.

A Christmas Story

Sure, I'd had too much wine and not enough
of the Advent hope that candles are lit for;
and I'll confess up front, I was without charity
for our guest who, glassed in behind those black,
small, rectangular frames, reminded me
of those poems that coldly arrange a puzzle
of non sequiturs to prove again how language
is defective and life leads to nothing more
than dead ends. So, after a night of wondering
if our never-more-than-hardly-surprised guest,
a young professor whose field of expertise
seemed to be ironic distance, would give
a moment's thought, as he took apart everyone's
unexamined stances, to how and why his own
might be constructed, I blurted out a story
over our Christmas dinner dessert, about
Aleksander Wat, how the Polish poet,
taken one day from his Soviet prison
to see a local magistrate, stood in the sun,
reveling in its warmth on his face and arms
and hands; as he took in the beauty
of a woman in a light green dress, he knew
he would soon be back in his prison cell.
He never forgot, he said, the irony of
his freedom, and yet he felt, standing there,
something like a revelation, the autumn day
surging in those silly puffiest white clouds,
and a hardly bearable blue sky, and the bell

of a bicycle ringing, and some people
laughing in a nearby café, and that woman,
her bare languid shoulders turning in the sun—
it was all thrilling, achingly alive, a feast
happening right there on the street between
the prison and a government office, nothing else
mattering, not even the moment he knew
was coming, and arrived, right on schedule,
when he stood woodenly before the magistrate.
And when I had finished, my face flushed,
my guest looked at me with astonishment,
unable to process where so much emotion
had come from, and then asked, calmly as ever,
what I meant when I'd used the word *revelation*.

A Dog's Nose

Muzzle tilted to the wind, nostrils flaring,
lips parted—a golden retriever just like ours
seemed to live on air this morning
when I walked the beach.
Now, alone and bored, I'm looking things up
on the Internet and find that
a dog's nasal membrane, if unfolded,
would be as large as a man's handkerchief.
And for what?—traces of urine, old turds,
a female gone by hours ago.
Just three weeks apart and already
I'm afraid I've lost your scent.

A thousand miles away
in my little writer's studio, I'm thinking of you
at home. I'm getting nothing done,
unless you count what I've learned
by Googling. Here's something
Heraklitus said about smell in the afterlife—
psyches there, with no means to see
or call or hear each other, find one another
by smell alone. If you were here,
I'd breathe you in, memorize your smell.
I'd train myself until I developed a dog's nose.
And if there is an afterlife, I vow,
even if it takes an eternity, to sniff my way
to you who, I trust, will be on my trail.

After Love

Our opened mouths close,
but the soft boundary
of our bodies remains porous
for a while longer.

An exchange keeps going on
between the darker afternoon light
inside and the brighter
light outside. The day is

loosening its hold. Birds flash
across the windows, unidentified.
We are still not back
from wherever it is we went.

We have grown old together.
Lying here so still,
so softened, our bodies
reach across a silence

that our minds, which keep
the door shut tightly
to our final separation,
cannot cross. Just now,

satisfied, spent, our bodies
seem to say that some day
we will not need
these pleasures any more,

that not being will be
as good as being. How can
I possibly imagine that,
save for this lying here,

the sheets pulled up
to cover our shoulders,
the two of us almost asleep,
our bodies nearly weightless.

Mint

This morning's rain roused
root smells of dirt and flowers
and now the sun
is tugging blue sky from
between some clouds.
I take hold of a sprig of mint,
crush it in my hands,
and wave it under my nose,
breathing in—a ritual
of sorts I have performed
for some thirty odd years
since coming to this house,
its wall-side garden overtaken
by mint planted, the former owner
told me, probably more
than a century ago to cure
indigestion and headache.

I toss a few minty leaves
in ice tea now and then,
or a bourbon around the time
of the Derby, but mostly
I just break open a few leaves
and let myself be dazzled
by the clean, sweet smell,
believing for a moment
that the past can be present
again, and history says more

than nothing lasts, and somehow
my life, unfinished, uncertain,
like a secret inside a secret,
is part of what is, like this mint,
pulled upward by the light,
by the day which only knows
again and again, to begin.

Reconfigurings

Holsteins in twos and threes,
weightless or earthbound as they pass
into and out of ground fog
rising from grass nearly tall enough
for a first cutting—I'm trying to walk out
of my grief, a nephew dead at thirteen.

From the fields' crown, May greens
are firming up on the hillsides,
and, above, clouds tumbling west to east
that make me think of Constable
and the handful of paintings he made
while his tubercular wife was dying.

Full sun now. A hard clarifying light
sharpens an edge on each tree branch,
each new leaf. The hills, too small
for names, run on like waves, dotted
here and there with houses—one worth
over a million, one hardly livable.

Nothing makes more sense from up here.
Getting up or staying in bed, eating
or not eating—every choice seems
arbitrary now, my sister-in-law told me.
These clouds seem so completely here,
and yet are constantly reconfiguring

themselves, unmappable shorelines
that keep opening and closing off
vast stretches of sky. When he painted,
Constable said he could smell
his wife's exhaustion on his hands.
The canvases record what occurred

each day, as if there were nothing more
he could do: the wet sand, hard-packed
and stony beside a sea tossed
with whitecaps; a few people dawdling
in the faint sunlight; the changing sky
streaked with rushing silvery-red clouds.

Night Walk

I'd started out with the last little runs
of thrush song, but soon I couldn't tell
where any one tree began or ended.
Leaves turned over and over, worry beads
in the small breeze and, above a field,
bats harrowed the deepening dark.
A dog's bark slit the silence that kept
filling in blank spaces. I saw the pond's
smoked glass give back the night
staring at itself, assured of its endlessness,

and I could not tell if what I felt was only
the fear that came with the pressing down
of wooded dark, or if it was more
the aftereffects of an article I'd read
about a recently found Auschwitz officer's
photo album. Sample snapshots showed
game-hunting trips, companionable
dogs, young women secretaries, wine,
and accordion sing-a-longs: Nazi officers
at a nearby retreat center taking their pleasure.

Not one sign that the men at their leisure—
leaning, say, against a terrace railing
eating blackberries—were affected
by their work. I wanted to file
the facts away under *banality of evil,*
and yet I could not, those pictures

turning upside down all those moments
of ordinary happiness I depend on . . .
When I came out of the woods, my neighbor's
floodlights picked up my motion, splayed
my shadow across the grass.

Ox-Pull Contest

Woodstock Fair

Flanks sweaty, teams of dust-covered oxen pull
sledges of cement weights
that get heavier with each success.

The oxen do what they do—bear
the burden—but bored and just a little miffed
by the unfairness of this contest
I'm all too unfairly connecting to myself,
I'm dredging up poems—

Stevens's Ox of the imagination
turning banality into poetry
and then the prescient oxen Hardy longed for,
his heavy beasts so lightly kneeling
in recognition of the child on Christmas Eve.

Christ, who wouldn't love the calm
of these creatures as they take up the yoke
of our desires, stepping forward to pull
what is heaped behind them?

When I try to find the animal in me
who might do its best
to budge what will not be budged,
then walk away untroubled,
all I can think of are those cement weights,
piled up now and dragged by the winning team
barely a foot or so at a time.

If I were Keats, perhaps I could see them
as the heavy stuff we must learn to bear
in the school of our soul-making;
but I can't find a lesson here—

each of these blocks of cement remains
just another gray weight that's added
to the load and which, dutifully,
this last pair of harnessed oxen takes on
for what will be one final pull,
the weight unmovable.

Composition in B Flat for Alligator

By late March, when the water dries up
in the swamps and the sprinkler systems
work overtime to keep the grass
the fashion statement it's required to be,
some alligator, squeezed out
of the mud, finds a sewer tunnel
and turns up inside the walls of Audubon Bay.

For the first day or two after the alligator
takes up residence at the water hazard
on the 15th green, club members tell stories—
biblical in proportion—of the monstrous girth
of its torso, the mountain range
of its back, the picket-fence scales of a tail
that moves like the breaking up of continents.

And yet by the third day, its *eyelids of morning*
have remained mostly shut and the beast
appears to be laughing, having itself
some private little Mesozoic chuckle.
In four days it's a nuisance, talk turning
to the alligator's incessant nightly bellowing
like some lovesick cow, then to tranquilizer guns.

Over lunch, when someone jokes
that alligators respond to the pitch of B flat,
Elizabeth suggests that Charles play his cello
just outside the gates. Everyone's chiming in—

a time for the concert, lawn chairs, gin and tonics—
when, unannounced, animal control shows up,
lassoes the Leviathan, and carts him off

for relocation. Once again the stately herons
patrol the shoreline. And the outdoor speakers
at the clubhouse playing the Righteous Brothers
provide everyone with that ever-loving feeling
as they listen to the agreeable pock
of tennis balls, and the thwack of a golf ball
headed straight down the groomed fairway.

Piano

No one could say how it came to be there,
on an islet of sand just above high tide
one morning—a grand piano left
for some Crusoe to make use of.
The picture in the paper—a bird's eye view
from one of those eye-in-the-sky helicopters—
makes it seem like a *New Yorker* cartoon
looking for a caption, or a piano looking
for a gull to plink a one-note concert
by John Cage. It could be an installation
by an unknown artist who's waiting
for someone to get what the piano is
saying. Or just a late-in-the-night prank
of buzzed college kids
looking for some music in their lives.

No answers were ever found.
Miami officials decided to let it be
a roosting place for gulls and pelicans.
Last night I dreamed I was fishing around
the little island where the piano sits.
Drifting close, I kept hearing the words
of songs I'd forgotten, but it wasn't the songs
that mattered; it was all the old questions
that were suddenly pressing again—
Where did it come from? Why was it here?
What did it mean? The sun was hot, the sky

so intensely blue I could barely face it.
I wasn't catching anything and, as usual,
only silence was answering the big questions,
but I felt alive, really alive, tuned again
to what is here without explanation.

In It

I'm watching a wall
of fast-moving gray-blue clouds
turn into a door the sun walks through
on this windy 29th day of October.

It walks down the yellowing hillside
and right up to a pair of scrub locusts,
which are of no importance at all
and yet, wired up with bittersweet's

red and yellow, seem just now to be
electrified by the light that just keeps coming,
crossing the street, extending itself
so that I am standing in it as well,

the skin on my face growing warmer.
I close my eyes and then, as if I have been
sleeping in a strange place, I let the light
wake me and tell me where I am.

Mid-Winter Emerson

Six weeks at a sunny writers' retreat
and now I'm descending in snow.
Passengers are shutting down their laptops.
When we land, they'll start up their cell phones
and chatter will reign: arrival, baggage,
meeting places. I shut my eyes, and return
to Emerson's journals, his belief
we were made for ecstasy and his fear
of just that; most days he grounded himself
in a miscellany of chores and the weather.

Midway through his life, he wrote about
finding himself on a stair, with steps below,
but many more above, climbing out of sight,
unreachable because of the sleep clouding
our eyes even when we're awake.
To climb, all he needed to do was walk outside
and be startled by a blue jay's alarm,
or the way its jay blue breaks through
the gray and white stillness of January . . .

We've landed. I collect my things and myself.
Emerson always knew how it would go—
that knock at the door, more than likely,
Henry, come to town to drag him away
to God knows what, and he, book and house
bound, making excuses for the work he must do

on a talk about the narrow passageway
between insanity and fat dullness, shoehorned
between two worlds, as he is now, in my hand,
among all of us rushing to get home or to get away,
moving up and down the airport escalators.

In the corner of an antique store
it hung by a nail, this water-stained,
frayed-edge chart, ingenious
at getting twenty-six birds—
from chimney swift to chipping sparrow,
all life-sized—on 27 x 42 inches.
Fuertes painted his stiff birds posed
in characteristic attitudes
on a convenient streamside dead tree, on reeds,
and on the wing in the background sky.

After I bought the chart and hung it
near the stairs, I found almost all twenty-six
are right here, going by
at various times outside my window.
Seeing the little golden crown on a kinglet,
or the tail-splash of red that sets off
the catbird's silky grey, puts me in good cheer.
And there's the sudden paradise of intimacy
when I turn my binoculars towards a house wren
nesting under the skewed lid of my propane tank.

None of this is life-changing
or halts the numbing dailiness of chores,
but since I hung this chart of birds,
I've come to think that what we know of our lives
often has nothing to do with understanding,

but with some accidental loveliness
we put our hopes in, the excess, say,
of a thrush fluting its elongated *ee—oo—lay;*
or the way a flock of goldfinches
yellows the air they fly through without asking.

No-Name Pond

It's a simple thing—
this stacking of stones at water's edge—
but what little I know
about cairns can't explain these,
which certainly do not mark a burial site
or the summit of anything;

and no one piled them in reverence
to something large and sublime,
though the eye of this pond, winking in the light,
is pretty; and, certainly, no one needs direction here—
it's one way in and one way out
to this pond beyond the larger Goose Lake.

Still, there's a miniature city
of fifty or so stone towers,
maybe six to twenty inches in height,
some just one stone on another,
some clearly ambitious, architectural,
as if the countless paddlers who paddled here
had answered a temporary call
to add their stones to those who'd come before.

I'm mostly a restorer, putting back
a few stones tumbled by time,
and thinking of the people who, like myself,
might have enjoyed an afternoon like this one—
light plashing down, the sway
of shoreline birches—
a kind of temporary amnesty from the daily war
of keeping up with upkeep.

Maybe all these cairns are just a way of saying
it was good to be here,
to watch flycatchers and kingbirds,
a heron that kept flying off
and circling back to the place it left
once I'd paddled by. Good to bring
a few stones together, and come to know,
so casually as I paddle off,
that, most likely, I'll never be back.

Acknowledgments

I am grateful to the following journals, which published many of these poems, sometimes in slightly different versions:

Alabama Literary Review: "In It"
Anglican Theological Review: "Kafka's Fence"
Artful Dodge: "Night Walk"
Big City Lit: "A Beginning"
Chautauqua Literary Journal: "Fall Cleaning, Windows
     Mostly," "Belated Elegy, January 1, 2011"
The Common: "Homeward," "Buying a TV"
Christianity and Literature: "Mid-Winter Emerson"
Connotation Press: "Childhood Room"
Georgia Review: "Elegy for an Idea"
Hampden-Sydney Review: "Mid-winter, Florida,"
     "Realometer"
Hudson Review: "1964"
Image: "The Field," "After Love," "A Christmas Story,"
     "Bede's Sparrow"
Literature and Belief: "Angel"
Minnesota Review: "A Dog's Nose"
New Ohio Review: "Pelicans," "Still Listening"

Orion: "Massachusetts Audubon Chart No. 1, 1898,"
    "Watching Cranes, I Think of Camus"
Post Road: "Evolution"
Seminary Ridge Review: "Mint"
Sewanee Review: "Last Day," "Reconfigurings," "Amnesty,"
    "Sunset Time in Florida"
Southern Review: "Piano," "Studio"
Southern Poetry Review: "Composition in B Flat for
    Alligator," "Winter Evenings in Florida," "The
    Restorer," "No-Name Pond"
Spiritus: "Like a Dream," "Essence"
Tar River Poetry: "Ox-Pull Contest"
Upstreet: "Indian Pipe," "Arrival of the Gods"
Verdad: "December 17, 1831"
Vineyards: "Annunciation"

I'm also grateful to the Hermitage in Englewood, Florida, where I wrote a number of these poems. For their comments on the earliest versions of some of these poems and the manuscript, I thank Brad Davis, Gray Jacobik, and Robert McQuilken. I am grateful to Baron Wormser for his help with the book's arrangement; and, once again I am especially grateful to Jeffrey Harrison and William Wenthe, whose attention and skill have made so many of these poems better.

CavanKerry's Mission

CavanKerry Press is committed to expanding the reach of poetry to a general readership by publishing poets whose works explore the emotional and psychological landscapes of everyday life.

Other Books in the Notable Voices Series

Printing this book on 30-percent PCW and FSC certified paper saved 2 trees, 1 million BTUs of energy, 127 pounds of CO_2, 67 pounds of solid waste, and 524 gallons of water.

The text of this book was typeset in Bembo, a 1920s copy of a typeface first cut in the late 15th century by Francesco Griffo. The typeface was first used to produce a 1496 edition of poetry by Pietro Bembo; the 20th century version is named for him.